PLAINFIELD

NEW JERSEY'S HISTORY & ARCHITECTURE

JOHN GRADY AND DOROTHE POLLARD

4880 Lower Valley Road, Atglen, Pennsylvania 19310

Other Schiffer Books on Related Subjects:

Jersey City: A Monumental History, 978-0-7643-2638-7, $24.95
Princeton: History and Architecture, 978-0-7643-2626-4, $29.95
The Great Swamp: New Jersey's Natural Treasure, 978-0-7643-2822-0, $19.95

Copyright © 2008 by John Grady and Dot Pollard
Library of Congress Control Number: 2008926225

Designed by Stephanie Daugherty
Type set in Trajen Pro / Souvenir Lt Bt / Humanist 521 Bt Bold

ISBN: 978-0-7643-2915-9

Printed in China

Schiffer Books are available at special discounts for bulk purchases for sales promotions or premiums. Special editions, including personalized covers, corporate imprints, and excerpts can be created in large quantities for special needs. For more information contact the publisher:

Published by Schiffer Publishing Ltd.
4880 Lower Valley Road
Atglen, PA 19310
Phone: (610) 593-1777; Fax: (610) 593-2002
E-mail: Info@schifferbooks.com

For the largest selection of fine reference books on this and related subjects, please visit our web site at:
www.schifferbooks.com

We are always looking for people to write books on new and related subjects. If you have an idea for a book please contact us at the above address.

This book may be purchased from the publisher. Include $5.00 for shipping. Please try your bookstore first. You may write for a free catalog.

In Europe, Schiffer books are distributed by
Bushwood Books
6 Marksbury Ave.
Kew Gardens
Surrey TW9 4JF England
Phone: 44 (0) 20 8392-8585; Fax: 44 (0) 20 8392-9876
E-mail: info@bushwoodbooks.co.uk
Website: www.bushwoodbooks.co.uk
Free postage in the U.K., Europe; air mail at cost.

CONTENTS

ACKNOWLEDGEMENTS

The following people and organizations deserve thanks:

Harry Ailster; Ralph Attanasia; John P. Benson Archives; Brown family; Pat Butynski; Emilia Carlson; E. Gary Cleveland; Courier News; Archibald Cox family; Christopher Damien; F. Edgar Davis; Sophie Dickson; Thomas C. Diller; ERA Suburb Realty; Anne W. Finch; Lois B. Force; Barbara and Gordon Fuller; William T. Garrett; Robin Gates; Roger Gilman; Mary Vic and Victoria Griswold; Ken Gormley; Jesse Levine of the Historical Society of Plainfield; Earle W. Holley; Gail Hunton; Robert Jester; George Lane; Morgan Lawrence; Nancy Leeds; Richard Loosli; Diane Mahoney; Metuchen-Edison Historical Society; Lauren McCready; Louise and Guido Mino; Muhlenberg Hospital Auxiliary; Helen C. Nasmith family; Nancy Piwowar; Joseph H. Da Rold and Jessica M. Myers of the Plainfield Public Library; PNC Bank; Jean Roxburgh; William J. Santoriello; Gary F. Schneider; Julie and Tom Shortridge; Ann Swain and Michael Ruple of Swain Galleries; Ketan and Krushna Thakker; Michael J. Wroble; Frederich Wallace family; William Jenkins of the Wardlaw-Hartridge School

SPECIAL NOTE OF APPRECIATION...

Much of Plainfield's fascination lies in the layering of one century upon another. Our sincere gratitude for the photographers who have recorded this progression down through the years, and to the collectors who have compiled their work for the generations to come. The photographs by Reina Lawrence, recently donated by John Grady, have joined the enviable collection of eighteenth, nineteenth, and twentieth century photography in the archives of the Plainfield Public Library. Among the library's treasures are early images by Guillermo Thorn; an extensive collection by Paul Revere Collier, much of which has been donated by William T. Garrett; views from the 1930s by J. Lloyd Grimstead; current examples of the work of John Hoffman; and contemporary subject matter by Irving Georges. Warmest thanks to Robert Stone who captured present day images for this book and, in so many other capacities, quietly compensated for the authors' shortcomings.

INTRODUCTION

These are the homes we live in, many of which have sheltered several generations before us. We take as much pride in them as did their original owners, for the history they tell in brick and wood and stone is part of our heritage. Here, too, are the buildings in which we worship, learn, heal our wounds, buy our worldly goods, and conduct our daily business.

Our predecessors over three centuries have already written their chapters in the continuing saga of this city. We welcome the opportunity to participate in the story and add our footnotes at the bottom of the page.

CHAPTER ONE:
FIELD AND FARMHOUSE

Discovered in the archives of the Historical Society of Plainfield, an astonishing 1951 rendering by architect Charles H. Detwiller, Jr. of the post-1864, fully-Victorianized summer home of banker John S. Harberger illustrates Plainfield's storied past. Within this elaborate complex lies the humble, 1746, four-room farmhouse of pioneer Nathaniel Drake. *Courtesy of the Historical Society of Plainfield.*

The Lawrence photographs create a time capsule of daily life as Reina Lawrence knew it, from the minutiae of her domestic surroundings illustrated here by a view of her niece, Dorothea Dix Lawrence (left) and a friend at play, to the beauty of the countryside beyond the comfort of her home. The scenes that introduce this pictorial history of Plainfield have now passed into the realm of nostalgia.

Reina Lawrence's arrival in Plainfield coincided with a special niche in the city's history. Between 1684 and the end of the Civil War, only isolated rural homesteads, mills, and tiny crossroads hamlets marked community growth on the plain beneath the Blue Hills (Watchung Mountains). Now, in 1882, remaining farmland was being swallowed up by residential development spreading from the city's core. Lawrence, from her newly-built residence on Stelle Avenue, would have a grandstand view of change.

Landscapes from the Reina Lawrence family albums do not identify locations, but these are among the rural scenes recorded for posterity...while poised on the brink of oblivion. As early as the 1870s, farmland was fast disappearing in Plainfield. Residential development had already begun on a tract of land that was originally the Rogers Farm, part of which is now Library Park. Senator James Martine of Cedar Brook Farm had his 1717 plantation surveyed and plotted in 1882, and Randolph Stelle was offering home sites in the mile-square acreage surrounding his old homestead. *Courtesy of Plainfield Public Library – Plainfield, New Jersey.*

Reina Lawrence's photographs illustrate the pastoral atmosphere of field and farm surrounding her adopted home. She wrestled the heavy, cumbersome camera equipment of her day into a cart or buggy to capture what remained of an environment she treasured. The simple, uncomplicated facades of early homesteads with their tiny knee wall windows (often called belly or eyebrow windows), the sturdy barns and stables, carriage houses, windmills, corncribs, and outhouses were soon to be changed beyond recognition. *Courtesy of Plainfield Public Library – Plainfield, New Jersey.*

By 1890, David Hand owned all the land on Leland Avenue, from Seventh Street to Cushing Road, and plans for development were on the horizon. Netherwood Heights was already occupied in 1895, with roads paving the way to building sites. In 1899, Muhlenberg Hospital's Board of Governors purchased pasture close to the eighteenth century FitzRandolph farmhouse for its new hospital. This unidentified dwelling, from the Lawrence album, was still holding its ground as progress marched toward its doorstep. *Courtesy of Plainfield Public Library – Plainfield, New Jersey.*

The home and wind-mill crowned farm buildings recorded here and on the preceding page by Reina Lawrence reappear, little changed, in a 1933 photograph identified as the Melick house in *Images of America – Edison* by Stacy E. Spies. The venerable dwelling stands today on Inman Avenue behind the Plainfield Country Club grounds, near Wardlaw-Hartridge School. Its site is part of the original Plainfield Plantation settled by John Barclay in 1684, south of the Cedar Brook. The Plainfield grant, covering most of what is now South Plainfield, was sold by the Barclays to Woodbridge Quaker John Laing in 1692. *Courtesy of Plainfield Public Library – Plainfield, New Jersey.*

Visiting this pre-revolutionary homestead must have been a special treat for Reina Lawrence. Her camera recorded not only the dwelling, but the pervasive atmosphere of a workaday farmyard. The site has been identified as the early grant of John Blackford, which extended along today's Woodland Avenue on a map of 1776 into what would become South Plainfield. It would be rewarding to imagine Lawrence sharing a cup of milk straight from the springhouse with the cheerful woman on the threshold. *Courtesy of Plainfield Public Library – Plainfield, New Jersey.*

In *Images of America – South Plainfield*, Richard Veit pinpoints John Blackford's plantation house as across the Bound Brook in what is now the Samptown section of South Plainfield, near the 1762 structure familiar to Plainfielders as "the second Drake house," and close to the old Samptown cemetery. Family ties were even closer than family farms might have been in Colonial days, for Isaac Drake and Hannah Blackford were the parents of Nathaniel Drake for whom the "Plainfield" Drake house was raised beside the Green Brook. *Courtesy of Plainfield Public Library – Plainfield, New Jersey.*

Gail Hunton's thoroughly-researched 1985 "Survey of Historic Building Resources for the City of Plainfield" describes the prevailing architectural style of the first half of the eighteenth century as one-and-one-half story, one-room deep dwellings called English cottages. A variation of the style, circa 1800-1830, can still be found on New Street, close to the city's center. The passing years have left their mark; here a nineteenth century porch, there a twentieth century door, yet it is recognizable for what it truly is — a legacy from the past. *Courtesy of Earle W. Holley.*

Nothing could have been more relaxing than a fine meal before a blazing hearth in an old Plainfield farmhouse. Such are the memories of those who fondly recall the pleasure of dining at the Clara Louise Tea Room on East Front Street. Former patrons still remember the picket gate, waitresses dressed in colonial garb, and beautiful rear gardens running down to Tier's Pond. *Courtesy of the Brown family.*

Clara Louise Brown's tea room charmed patrons at this location from 1929 to 1949, when the building was demolished to construct Bamberger's Department Store, now a mini mall called Plainfield Plaza. On Thanksgiving Day 1942, the bounteous, six-course menu offered roast turkey, oysters, vichysoisse, Roquefort salad, lemon sherbet, and brandied mince pie for two bucks a head. *Courtesy of the Brown family.*

Stripped to the basics, this circa 1780-1850 home on Elmwood Place proved irresistible to curious passersby back in the 1990s. A larger variation of the English cottage, it closely resembles both the Blackford and FitzRandolph farmhouses. Shorn of its nineteenth century porch, the building appears to have been slated for restoration. Sadly, fire intervened before the house could make its way into the twenty-first century. *Courtesy of Christopher Damien.*

The oldest documented European-built dwelling in what is now the City of Plainfield became home to Thomas Gordon on Christmas Day in 1684. The settler from Scotland sold his plantation to William Webster, Jr. in 1717, and Gordon's log cabin was replaced by the tiny, frame English cottage that still stands as the west wing of Cedar Brook Farm on Brook Lane. Webster's eighteenth century home appears here as it did in a sketch from a Muhlenberg Hospital Auxiliary designer show house program in 1988. From such small beginnings, the farmhouse expanded, one section per century, to the size we see today. *Courtesy of Muhlenberg Hospital Auxiliary.*

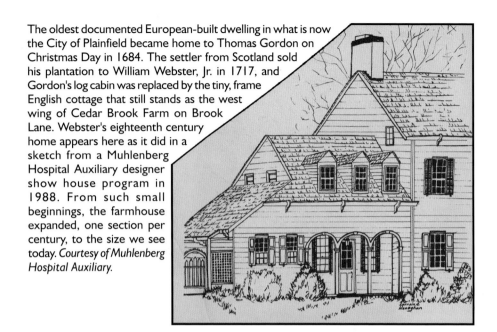

Four generations of Websters continued to farm the plantation, operate the mill on the Green Brook, supply the Revolutionary encampment, provide land for the Quaker meetinghouse, and enlarge their living quarters, completing the central portion of the house by 1800. Early in the nineteenth century, the family moved to Canada, selling the farm on Cedar Brook to David L. Dodge. Dodge shared his home for a time with his daughter, Quaker poetess Elizabeth Stedman, her second husband W. B. Kinney, minister to France under President Pierce, and grandson, Edmund Clarence Stedman.

Daniel Martine purchased the venerable farmstead in 1858. Five years later, management of the estate passed to his fourteen-year-old son. From that time on, James Martine's livelihood was farming; his abiding passion, politics. The combination earned him the affectionate title of Plainfield's farmer-orator. Martine's political ambitions were finally realized during his term in the United States Senate from 1911-1917, and in June of 1912, he fired the first legislative salvo in the battle to preserve Monticello as a memorial to Thomas Jefferson.

James E. Martine.

In true Jeffersonian style, Martine's hospitality was widely known and readily accepted. It is believed the east wing ballroom was added to the homestead during his tenure to facilitate increasing social obligations. Farmer Jim might even qualify as Plainfield's first historic preservationist, long before the movement gained the prestige it holds today. Entering the twenty-first century, Cedar Brook Farm is lovelier than ever. All of its owners have responded to its charm with appropriate care and pride.

In this nineteenth century photograph, the middle section of the tripartite Stelle Farmhouse on Central Avenue peeps through a break in the shrubbery. Dated 1803, this portion of the structure may actually be settler James Manning's 1729 English cottage, which appears on a map of 1776 on or near this site. The name of the last Stelle descendant to live here, Randolph Manning Stelle, more than hints at a family connection. The farmhouse has survived its centuries by adapting to changing tastes with the passage of years. *Courtesy of Barbara and Gordon Fuller.*

The original wing of the Stelle Farmhouse presents itself in a familiar role—the first-stage section of a larger dwelling. Tucked between a sturdy 1855 farmhouse and a lean-to at the east end of the complex, a three-bay, center door facade with a raised roof and second-story window mark its location in this 1926 photograph. Graceful sidelights have been restored and an ornamental fan above the entrance is complimented by a lattice surround. Today, as in the past, the eighteenth century portion of the building is still the heart of the house — it is the kitchen. *Courtesy of Courier News – Bridgewater, New Jersey.*

This was the home of Edward FitzRandolph, farmer, patriot, provisioner of the Blue Hills Fort, guide to General George Washington in his initial trip to Washington's Rock, and head carpenter when the Friends meetinghouse was raised on Peace Street (Watchung Avenue) in 1788. The circa 1717 homestead's kinship to the dwelling on Elmwood Place and the Blackford Farm is clear. It has not only survived almost three centuries, but has been maintained with integrity throughout its long history. *Courtesy of Michael J. Wroble.*

The last FitzRandolphs to spend their lives on the old farmstead were Amanda (b. 1873) and Anna Mabel (b. 1882). The farm passed from family hands during World War II. Eye-catching at any season of the year, the homestead on Randolph Road seems especially evocative of the past in winter when, a candle alight in every window, it glows like a ruby in the snow. *Courtesy of Earle W. Holley.*

Could this photograph, recently discovered in the Reina Lawrence albums, be an early view of the 1690-1720 Lampkin Farmhouse on Terrill Road? Found among the pages containing identifiable photographs of other Plainfield landmarks, the image opens the door to speculation, but nothing more. The house displays similarities with the next photograph, as well as those taken by Gail Hunton, circa 1975, that follow. *Courtesy of Plainfield Public Library – Plainfield, New Jersey.*

Gail Hunton's photographs capture the Lampkin farmhouse as it stands today, complete with classical modillion cornices and porch trim, the porch now even more impressive with its square, Greek Revival posts. But where is the object of our quest, the modest cottage of Plainfield's Colonial past? *Courtesy of Gail Hunton.*

It's here, still here, almost completely concealed within the whole by additions and alterations. Below the center chimney lies the homestead's original open-hearth fireplace and bake oven, proof of the building's early origin. Possibly the oldest survivor of Plainfield's seventeenth century Scottish settlement, the farmhouse cradles its secrets in peace. *Courtesy of Gail Hunton.*

In this verified image of the Lampkin Farmhouse, flanking dormers with arched windows mirror the central cross gable. A simple shed roof protecting the entrance has been replaced by a more generous bracketed porch with decorative columns. Brackets also trim the eaves, lending weight and substance to the home's exterior.

Clockwise from top left: The 1746 kitchen of the Drake House, just off the central core of the original four-room farmhouse, appears just as it did when Nathaniel Drake brought his bride to her new home. The wide cooking hearth survives intact. At that time, only minimal comforts were supplied. While no record exists of a well or cistern beneath the floorboards such as ones found at the Stelle and FitzRandolph homesteads, the brook is near at hand. *Courtesy of the Historical Society of Plainfield.*

The Queen Anne dining room, 1746-1790, replicates its appearance during the Revolutionary War when General Washington chose the Drake House as his command post during the Battle for the Short Hills on June 26-27, 1777—the battle after which Lord Cornwallis withdrew his forces from New Jersey, never to return. The ceiling beams and fireplace bricks are original to the house, but the mantel and corner cupboard are replacements taken from other pre-Revolutionary homes in the area during the room's restoration. *Courtesy of the Historical Society of Plainfield.*

The Washington Bedroom commemorates General Washington's visits to the Drake House during his trips to the Blue Hills Fort and Encampment on Cornelius and Frederick Vermeule's plantation just across the Green Brook. According to Phoebe Drake, a daughter of Nathaniel, the General rested here on his cot between strategy meetings with his staff. In days to come, the Drakes kept the room sacred to Washington's memory and refused to let the children play there. The bed serves as a display piece for the museum's lovely collection of period quilts. *Courtesy of the Historical Society of Plainfield.*

The Empire Parlor, circa 1860, is more accurately a graceful blending of Late Empire-Early Victorian design suitable for a gentleman farmer and represents the period when the Drakes' 188-year tenure was drawing to a close. In 1864, it became the home of the John S. Harberger family, which enlarged and altered the little farmhouse over the next fifty-three years. The parlor's furnishings include an 1840 portrait of Nathaniel Drake, son of the builder. Elsewhere in the house are portraits of Cornelius Boice and family, also painted in 1840. Comparisons are inevitable. The Drakes' eighteenth century farmhouse has survived; the Boices' nineteenth century mansion has not, which is another tale for the telling. *Courtesy of the Historical Society of Plainfield.*

Sleepy Hollow is a relatively recent name for one of Plainfield's choice residential neighborhoods. Earlier, it was simply the Hand farm. William Hand's farmhouse (1750–1800) still stands on Leland Avenue, its west wing revealing the traditional cottage of settlement days now joined with a tower-like Victorian addition. Hand's sawmill, pond, barns, and stables were clustered in the vicinity of today's Sleepy Hollow Lane and Fernwood Avenue. Only the millpond remains, reminding a twenty-first century neighborhood of its eighteenth century origins.

Peterson's Farm on Cushing Road, built in 1910, stands today hardly a stone's throw from William Hand's eighteenth century homestead, sharing common destinies two centuries apart. Claus Peterson erected a barn in 1895, in which he lived while his home was being completed. A brick milk house appears between the barn and the house. Peterson's son, Peter, worked the land in later years and his grandson, Charles, now follows the family tradition on the sole remaining livestock farm in Plainfield — and in Union County. This land was subdivided during the twentieth century, but cows peacefully graze and eggs are still for sale beside ranches, bi-levels, and the last of Plainfield's urban farmhouses. Courtesy of Earle W. Holley.

CHAPTER TWO:
FREE THE GREEN BROOK

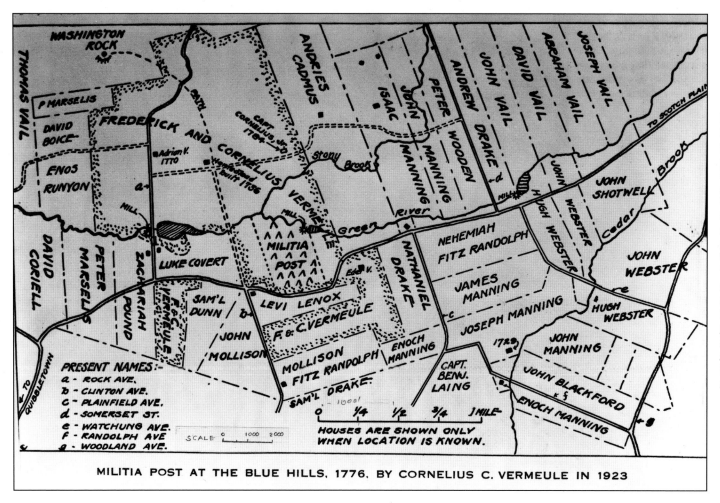

MILITIA POST AT THE BLUE HILLS, 1776, BY CORNELIUS C. VERMEULE IN 1923

In this reconstruction of Plainfield's seventeenth and eighteenth century plantations and the Blue Hills Fort and Encampment during the Revolutionary War, the millpond on the Green Brook lies in the upper right quarter of the map, at the joining of the Vail and Webster farms. The Green Brook and the mill it fueled would be stable components of the local landscape for many generations…constants in a world of change.
Map prepared by Cornelius C. Vermeule in 1923, from family records.

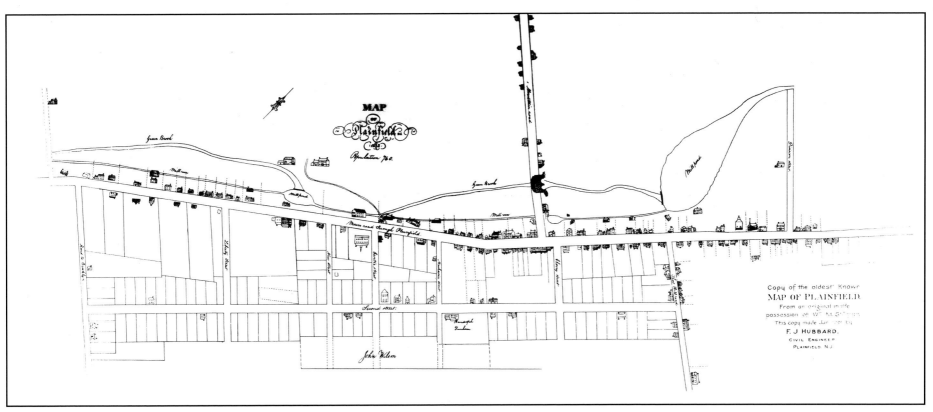

From the *Plainfield Herald*, published by Isaac Cole in October 1835, we learn, "The middle part of the house where John Wilson lives was the first frame house built in Plainfield, and this was put up in 1735, at which time there were none but log houses and Indian wigwams around." On Stillman's map of 1832, an increase in home sites is apparent and clearly shows the east-west expansion of the early mill town along Old York Road (Front Street) and the course of the Green Brook. Both townsfolk and travelers often called the village, "Pinchgut," because of its lateral development. For much of the city's history the growth pattern persisted, with the hat industry crowding the banks of the brook, residences replacing the hatters, and, eventually, commercial expansion overtaking the farms and country estates along the main thoroughfare.

In the crossroads village stretching east and west along the banks of the millstream, the shops and homes of hatters jostled for position. Access to water for bleaching and dying fabrics was critical from 1808, when John Wilson first opened his shop, to the industry's peak in mid-century. It's enlightening to see Equal Opportunity Employment in effect at such an early date, at least between the sexes.

First National Bank, chartered April 25, 1864, shortly after the establishment of the National Bank Act, numbered hatters among the businessmen on its Board of Directors. Front row, left to right, William McDowell Coriell (hatter), Phineas M. French (mill owner), Charles Potter, President; second row, Frank Runyon, Cashier, Daniel R. Randolph (merchant), William M. Stillman, Mulford Estil, J. Wesley Johnston. These names echo throughout Plainfield's history. *Courtesy of PNC Bank.*

Post-revolutionary travelers along the dusty stagecoach route to Scotch Plains could not fail to notice an impressive new homestead just beyond the edge of the village. It piques our interest to this day. Gail Hunton describes the farmhouse as, "The best example of the Federal Style in Plainfield, and…one of the ten oldest documented houses in the city." A period portico shelters a doorway with a four-light transom and dainty sidelights. The exterior is elegant, refined, and in pristine condition. Proof of an early construction date? A beehive oven remains in its original basement location. *Courtesy of Plainfield Public Library – Plainfield, New Jersey.*

The Federal Period in American history was not a peaceful era. A new nation was struggling to establish itself and gain permanence. Nothing was tranquil, except the architecture of the period, now rising above the basic requirements of Colonial days. Erected between 1800-1825, Plainfield's Federal House expresses the style of its day unchanged.

In 2008, the Federal House remains inviolate—a rare example untouched by time. Converted for professional use, it is still in good hands and serves its owners well, but the landscape it once overlooked is gone beyond recall. *Courtesy of Earle W. Holley.*

19

GREEN BROOK, PLAINFIELD, N. J.

VIEW FROM WEST END AVE. BRIDGE, PLAINFIELD, N. J.

Green Brook, Plainfield, N. J.

It really looked like this. Honest. These postcards, mailed from Plainfield between 1908 and 1910, frame an open countryside. Channeled on its passage through town, the Green Brook was still free to follow its natural course outside the confines of the business district. The time would come when open fields would be cordoned off into tiny parcels, with street signs, telephone poles, power lines, Plainfield Municipal Utility Authority containers, and satellite dishes punctuating the landscape. But not yet. Not yet.

The uncomplicated rectangular box that characterized the English cottage was being replaced by more substantial structures as growth progressed along East Front Street. Originally the Plainfield Seminary, founded by E. Dean Dow in 1833, and later the Fairchild School for Boys, this building was purchased by Cornelius Boice in 1840. Plainfield's first lawyer set about transforming it into his vision of a country estate. Soon, a classic Greek temple with pedimented gable and fluted, Ionic columns emerged within a sheltering allée of trees. *Courtesy of PNC Bank.*

BELOW: In an early twentieth century photograph, the house, while still lovely, appears stark and ill at ease. The trees look blighted, buildings encroach on either side, and the atmosphere is one of neglect. During World War I, the government utilized the mansion as an armory, and time has not been kind. One man's vision of perfection was demolished in the 1920s—victim to the city's flourishing commercial district. *Courtesy of the Historical Society of Plainfield.*

The palatial Greek Revival residence of Phineas M. French, last owner-operator of the old mill (1859-1901), fared no better. Erected at the corner of Somerset and Pearl Streets in North Plainfield, just across Green Brook from the mill, it could not withstand the development of the downtown. One can imagine French striding daily across the stream, dividing home from business. But when this beautiful icon failed the test of time, two communities shared in the loss. *Courtesy of the Historical Society of Plainfield.*

In the earliest documented image of the old millpond by Holme's photographist from New York and dated 1858, the barn, sheds, dock, fences, and springhouse behind the Boice Estate are viewed from the opposite bank. Beyond the rear wing of the mansion rise the roofline and chimneys of the main block, almost lost in the mists of time. This dreamlike setting disappeared beneath asphalt and macadam in the twentieth century, but what scenic beauty might be restored to the center of the community if municipal and state authorities banded together to free the Green Brook in the twenty-first century. *Courtesy of the Historical Society of Plainfield.*

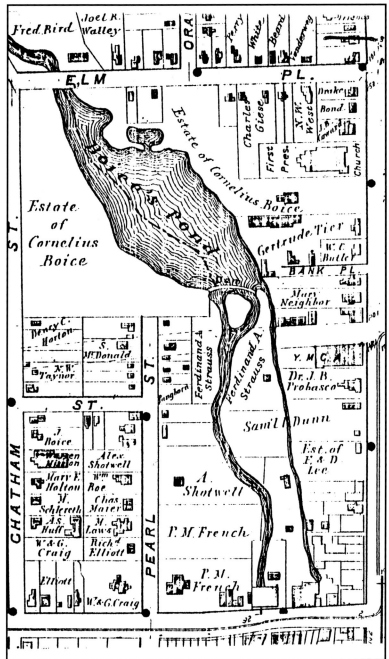

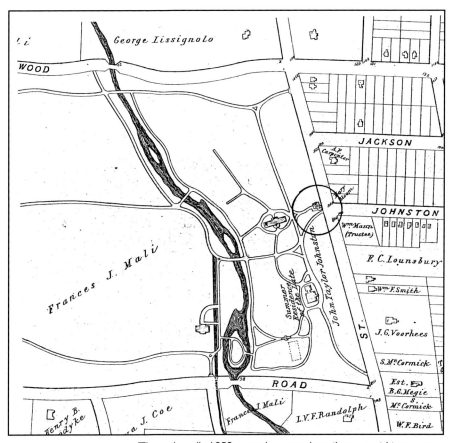

The P. M. French residence, its adjoining mill, and Corneliuvs Boice's property appear on an 1878 F. A. Dunham map of the city. The pond is familiar, by whatever name it might be called, as the millpond of colonial days. Successively christened with the name of whomever owned the land on which it lay, in the latter 1800s, John Tier claimed the honor by virtue of his popular ice cream pavilion. So shall it be remembered.

The railroad's 1852 annual report describes a rapid increase in passengers to Plainfield "to which numbers now remove in the summer with their families," and John Taylor Johnston did just that, purchasing more than one hundred acres on both sides of the brook for his rural retreat. His estate, spreading east along Front Street, was detailed in F. A. Dunham's 1894 "Atlas of the City of Plainfield." Called "Netherwood" after Johnston's ancestral home in Scotland, the name resurfaces today in a commercial neighborhood, a train station, a vanished resort hotel, and a historic district.
Courtesy of Gail Hunton.

John Taylor Johnston, president of the Central Railroad of New Jersey until 1877, was ahead of his time in every sense of the word. Born in 1820, he graduated from the University of the City of New York at the age of nineteen, obtained a law degree from Yale at twenty-three, and assumed the presidency of the railroad when he was only twenty-eight.

23

A pair of photographs from *Plainfield and Vicinity In Pictures* contrast with postcard views of similar vintage. The Green Brook was a popular postcard subject and, today, examples are eagerly sought by collectors, often exclusively. Every crossing of the brook boasted its own bridge design, no two alike. The postcard view focuses on Leland Avenue's rustic bridge. The photograph captures the grounds of Frederick G. Meade on East Front Street. *Courtesy of Courier News – Bridgewater, New Jersey.*

John Taylor Johnston's summer compound included a home for his daughter, Frances, wife of the Belgian Consul General Pierre Mali. The Mali home is reproduced here, circa 1926, from the *Courier-News* publication *Plainfield and Vicinity In Pictures*. After Johnston's death in 1893, the estate remained intact until 1936 when it was subdivided into building lots. The fairyland through which the Green Brook flowed yielded to reality. All that marks the spot is an enchanting gatehouse. *Courtesy of Courier News – Bridgewater, New Jersey.*

24

In another view from the *Courier-News* 1926 publication, we visit "Kenjockery," the home and gardens of John A. Staats on Mountain Avenue, north of the Green Brook. Contemporary with the photograph of the Mali home, it weaves its own spell as one of many idyllic spots along the winding stream during this period in the city's history. *Courtesy of Courier News – Bridgewater, New Jersey.*

The 1923 edition of A. Van Doren Honeyman's *History of Union County* tells us Lewis V. F. Randolph, "built wonderful gardens, planting hundreds of varieties of rare and beautiful trees, flowers, and plants." Honeyman was not alone in his opinion. Both the postcard and the photograph offer views of "Blojocamavi," the Randolph estate on East Front Street near Farragut Road. *Courtesy of Courier News – Bridgewater, New Jersey.*

VIEW FROM FARRAGUT ROAD,
PLAINFIELD, N. J.

GARDENS OF PHIROZ SAKLATVALA

Ancient stone Fu dogs and a stone lantern guard the path to a sacred shrine at Saklatvala's "Gulestan" (Garden of Flowers). In this setting, Mary Pickford honors her ancestors in a scene from the 1915 film "Madame Butterfly," produced by Famous Players, later known as Paramount Pictures. Was this the first location shoot to take place in the Plainfields? Possibly, but it would not be the last. A precedent had been set. Cinematographers continue to be attracted to the area, most recently for the movie "Kinsey" in 2003. *Courtesy of the Plainfield Public Library – Plainfield, New Jersey.*

Birches, rhododendrons, mountain laurels, and ferns frame a pagoda in the gardens of Phiroz Saklatvala, Persian Consul General, at East Front Street and Leland Avenue. Saklatvala purchased the Leland family acreage in 1907, turning farmland into an oriental paradise. Under the guidance of architect Takeo Shiota, who later designed the Japanese garden at the Brooklyn Botanical Gardens, the Green Brook was diverted into several branches, flowing around two islands connected by seven bridges, one of which replicated the sacred bridge at Nikko. *Courtesy of the Historical Society of Plainfield.*

The rays of the setting sun trace a path across the Green Brook, highlighting the Saklatvala-Stillman home. The scene is prophetic. The site where Madame Butterfly fulfilled her selfless destiny gave way to the brick and masonry of an apartment complex called Stillman Gardens in 1962. *Courtesy of the Plainfield Public Library – Plainfield, New Jersey.*

Old sepia-toned photographs cause historians and preservationists to catch their breath. What has been discovered that will recall a moment from the past? The mode of dress suggests the 1930s, the period when Virginia and Albert Stillman purchased the Saklatvala estate. One scene features the Fu dogs near the site of Pickford's performance, and from there, the path to the major portion of the Japanese garden extends over a bridge to the North Plainfield bank of the stream at the rear of the five acre property. *Courtesy of the Historical Society of Plainfield.*

The scene changes. A companion photograph surveys a vista of massive entrance gates, lawn, abundant roses, a lily pond, and elegant garden furnishings, part of the Italian gardens at the front of the Saklatvala mansion on the Plainfield side of the Green Brook. The ambiance is now European formality, befitting the approach to a remodeled farmhouse of impressive dimensions. These are gardens watered by the Green Brook three quarters of a century ago. *Courtesy of the Historical Society of Plainfield.*

CHAPTER THREE:
EXTRAORDINARY PEOPLE, EXTRAORDINARY PLACES

"Every Thanksgiving… we'd go to New York, take the ferry at Liberty Street and then the steam train to Plainfield…The house was something. Lovely Irish maids right off the boat, Robert Collins the coachman, had a tall black silk hat!…" *Courtesy of Lauren McCready.*

The fabulous Netherwood Hotel occupied an entire city block at Belvidere Avenue and Denmark Road, providing a luxurious summer retreat for wealthy New Yorkers. On May 11, 1907, owner John Truell opened the newly christened Truell Hall for the season. A busy day ensued.

On May 11, 1907, the 11th regiment of the Grand Army of the Republic held its reunion. Commander Hand had double reason for celebrating since it coincided with his 50th wedding anniversary. Hand and his wife, Fannie Cushing, welcomed over three hundred guests, including Mayors Fisk and Smalley as well as the well-known New York journalist, Arthur Brisbane.

All that remains to identify the site of Plainfield's storied hostelry is a flight of stone steps ascending an ivied bank toward the crest where the gargantuan building once stood. Twentieth century homes now crown the heights where summer visitors spent halcyon days and danced beneath the light of lanterns after dark. *Courtesy of the Historical Society of Plainfield.*

English-born Job Male made his fortune in Jersey City developing and installing adjustable ferry slips. He became Plainfield's first mayor and a great philanthropist.

Job Male designed his own Crescent Avenue home as well as several other homes in the neighborhood. Male's home, now in a historic area, is an important transitional design incorporating elements of both the Italianate and Second Empire styles.

TIME
THE WEEKLY NEWSMAGAZINE

VAN WYCK BROOKS
He is rediscovering the American past.
(Books)

Plainfield's famous native son, Van Wyck Brooks, made his mark in the literary world as critic, editor, and cultural historian. His 1936 *The Flowering of New England* won the Pulitzer Prize in history. In later years, Brooks said that Plainfield, with its characters, would be good subject matter for a novel. However, Raymond Nelson, a biographer of Brooks, stated that "Plainfield retained permanently the power to depress him beyond tears."

Owner of the former Van Wyck Brooks house, Percy Stewart in his later years relaxing with his favorite German shepherd.

Percy Stewart's wife, Elinor Cochran Stewart was the daughter of Alexander Smith Cochran, the wealthy Yonkers carpet man. An acknowledged leader of society, Mrs. Stewart was active in many civic affairs. The Stewart's niece noted that more help than family lived in their magnificent mansion.

This handsome West Eighth Street house, owned by Van Wyck Brooks' wealthy maternal grandfather, was where the budding author spent his formative years. The home was later purchased by Percy and Elinor Stewart and doubled in size (as shown here). The inside was fitted out with the panels, walls, and ceilings from an ancient Scottish castle purchased from the Duveens. The end result caused a friend of Van Wyck Brooks to quip that the house was "colonial outside, baronial inside."

Percy Stewart's father, Walter Eugene Stewart, was one of the founders of the Plainfield Country Club and also served as the first treasurer to Crescent Avenue Presbyterian Church. His wife, Anne G. Leeper Stewart, had been raised in New York society and, according to her granddaughter, found aspects of Plainfield society "decidedly provincial."

Shown in a rare early image, Percy Hamilton Stewart, oldest of the three brothers, attended Yale and Columbia Law School, graduating with honors. He served as Mayor of Plainfield, State Highway Commissioner, and also in the House of Representatives, filling the vacancy left by the death of Ernest Ackerman.

At 6'2", Irving Stewart, seen here with the family dog Nip, was the tallest of the brothers. His service in World War I compromised his health. He later moved to Virginia where he became a writer for the *Gloucester County Gazette*.

Walter, the middle brother, graduated from Yale and became a cavalry lieutenant in the Spanish-American War. On his way home from the Philippines, he died suddenly in San Francisco.

In addition to serving as sergeant in the Union army, mayor of Plainfield, library and hospital trustee, world traveler, and director of the Illinois Central Railroad, L. V. F. Randolph found the time to lecture and author a book of poems entitled, *Survivals*. For many years, Mr. Randolph served as secretary to the Samuel J. Tilden estate, the lawyer/statesman from New York. One of Mr. Randolph's five daughters married Harry Keith White, an architect who designed many notable buildings in Plainfield.

The East Front Street home of Lewis and Emily Price Randolph was surrounded by lush gardens where rare plants and trees, both foreign and domestic, were planted. Alas, it is no more. *Courtesy of the Historical Society of Plainfield.*

Ernest Ackerman resided on West Eighth Street, one of Plainfield's grand esplanades. His home, still standing today, featured unusual stepped Flemish dormers.

ERNEST R. ACKERMAN.

An 1880 Plainfield High School graduate, Ernest Ackerman had interests in the Dragon Cement Manufacturing Company. Having served on the Plainfield Common Council, Ackerman went on to serve as state senator from 1905 to 1911. From 1919 until his death in 1931, Mr. Ackerman served in the United States Congress. After his death, a portion of his world-famous stamp collection was donated to the government.

Raised in Plainfield, Charles H. Smith became an architect and worked in the New York City office of Russell Sturgis, architectural editor of the *Century Dictionary*. By 1878, Smith had established his own practice with offices in New York and Plainfield. Many noteworthy homes in the area were designed by him.

In the 1890s, Charles Smith was the architect for this astounding home built for local attorney Craig Adams Marsh. Still standing and in the process of being restored, this West Eighth Street structure is a testament to all the wonderful things that can be accomplished with stone and wood.

The interior hall of the Marsh home is cast in the warm colors shed by a dome and series of stained glass windows.

George Endicott's residence was a mansarded roof fantasy. Its prominent location on the corner of West Seventh Street and Park Avenue made it a vulnerable target for the burgeoning downtown. In the 1920s, the house was replaced by the current Masonic Hall.

George Woodhull Endicott was a direct descendant of John Endicott, the first colonial governor of the Massachusetts colony. After moving to Plainfield in 1880, Endicott became established as the leading surgeon at Muhlenberg Hospital when it opened in 1881. As a member of the Board of Health, Endicott inaugurated many improvements in the city's sanitary conditions.

Charles Francis Abbott was a manager of the New York office of Warner Bros. Co., corset manufacturers. Mr. Abbott was interested in educational affairs and served on the school board. According to Mr. Abbott, one of his ancestors was a Tory and, if he had gotten his just desserts, there would have been no current Mr. Abbott.

The Abbott mansion stood on the corner of Central and Stelle Avenues. An unusual Shingle Style mansion with extensive grounds, the house eventually became a target for insensitive modern development and subdivision. Fortunately, its unique carriage house survived.

36

Plainfield photographer Paul Collier's family poses in front of their Second Empire style house on East Sixth Street. The lush vines and elephant ears lend an almost tropical aura to the setting. The Collier house was razed in the late 1970s.

Plainfield resident, ardent bicycle enthusiast, and architect who specialized in country homes, Mr. Augustus L. C. Marsh designed many fine residences in Plainfield. Marsh also designed public buildings such as the original YMCA and the Elks club.

Augustus Marsh designed many homes in the popular Shingle Style such as this modest but comfortable Madison Avenue home with its gambrel roof, two story bay, and rubble stone chimney.

Augustus Marsh moved easily from the modest to the magnificent as shown by this Stelle Avenue residence. This residence, now gone, was featured in a Scientific American Building Supplement and was described as a home in the modified Dutch Colonial style. The house featured doors of San Domingo mahogany; interior stairs displayed balusters in four different designs. The home had a frontage of 56' and the side was 38' exclusive of the piazza. Parts of the German valley stone fences that surrounded the property are the only testament to the home's existence. Four non-distinctive houses occupy the site.

John P. Benson, architect and artist, spent only ten years in Plainfield, but he left an awesome signature in the form of the many fine homes he designed for his fellow townsmen. *Courtesy of the John P. Benson Archives.*

Around 1897, John Benson built his own rather modest Shingle Style residence on Hillside Avenue. An unusual feature of the house was the exterior siding of wood shingles placed three in thickness with the butts laid 1/2" to weather. The house cost Mr. Benson $7,500.

When John Benson designed the shingle house next door to his own, a magazine article referred to the home as a "quaint and interesting little house." The Hillside Avenue homes had generous back yards that allowed for carriage barns and lovely private gardens.

In 1909, again on Hillside Avenue, John Benson designed this impressive Colonial Revival style home for Frederick and Grace Wallace. *Courtesy of the Shortridge and Wallace families.*

Frederick and Grace Wallace are caught on camera sharing a light-hearted moment. *Courtesy of the Shortridge and Wallace families.*

Grace Wallace and an unidentified companion share a quiet moment alongside the man-made pond in the Wallace garden. *Courtesy of the Shortridge and Wallace families.*

The Wallace house featured a front to back center hall with a graceful fan-lighted doorway, scenic wallpaper, and a broad spiral staircase. *Courtesy of the Shortridge and Wallace families.*

The paneled fireplace wall harks back to an earlier era. However, the flowered wallpapers, wall sconces, and round mahogany table set the time to the early twentieth century. *Courtesy of the Shortridge and Wallace families.*

In the days before prepared and frozen foods were available, kitchens were rooms of intensive labor. The kitchen was large, utilitarian, and simply arranged for maximum efficiency. *Courtesy of the Shortridge and Wallace families.*

This cozy, simply furnished room was labeled on the blueprints as the children's dining room. Maybe it isn't an idle phrase that children should be seen and not heard. *Courtesy of the Shortridge and Wallace families.*

41

When the J. P. Stevens Co. moved its offices to New York City, Horace Stevens relocated his family to Plainfield and had John Benson design this massive Shingle Style house for his family on Prospect Avenue. *Courtesy of Mary Vic Griswold.*

The Horace Stevens family pose in the garden of their Prospect Avenue home. Seated are Horace Nathaniel and Helen Coburn Stevens with their three children: Helen, Nathaniel, and Mary Vic. *Courtesy of Mary Vic Griswold.*

Lauren McCready's grandparents George Arthur and Harriet Efner Wheelock Strong had New York architects Rossiter and Wright build this yellow brick house on Central Avenue. Rear Admiral McCready remembered as a child: "The hall had melodious chimes to announce dinner, stained glass panels, gorgeous woodwork, banisters to slide down. It had old-fashioned gas lighting — pull this way or that to change the flame's light." *Courtesy of Lauren McCready.*

Rear Admiral Lauren McCready, one of the builders and founders of the United States Merchant Marine Academy "Kings Point," spent many days as a child at his grandparents' Plainfield home. He has been kind enough to share his photos and memories with us. *Courtesy of Lauren McCready.*

Architectural appointments carried the day in the front parlor. The ivy-laden arch leading to the conservatory was to be the setting for the wedding of one of the Strong daughters, Agnes.
Courtesy of Lauren McCready.

George Strong poses with two of his daughters, Effie and Agnes.
Courtesy of Lauren McCreaady.

The lady of the house, Harriet Strong, was a camera enthusiast and had her own darkroom on the second floor of the mansion. In this photo, an unnamed photographer captures Harriet taking a picture. *Courtesy of Lauren McCready.*

The son of the house, Malcolm Wheelock Strong, graduated from Stanford University and embarked on a harrowing sea voyage on the schooner, *Edw. R. West.* He recorded in his journal the events of the voyage during which the captain and his dog were washed overboard in a storm. Sitting on the Central Avenue porch, Malcolm peruses his diary. Later in California, Malcolm wrote moving picture plays for Universal Film Company. His career was cut short by his untimely death in 1916 in an automobile accident. *Courtesy of Lauren McCready.*

Agnes Strong and her husband Howard lived in this Italianate style house on Franklin Place. According to McCready, Agnes was quite a person. "She ordered her pet old Franklin car buried in the flower bed rather than see it go to the junkyard." *Courtesy of Lauren McCready.*

Agnes's Franklin Place home today. Words are inadequate!

46

Born in 1899, Dorothea Dix Lawrence eventually became known as the "ambassadress of music." She was a soprano of opera, concert, radio, and television. Tireless in her promotion of American music folklore, Lawrence traveled the world performing and lecturing. Lawrence's hobby was collecting vintage Christmas cards, which today can be seen at the Philadelphia Athenaeum. Many of the singer's music related papers are housed in the Library of Congress. *Courtesy of Morgan Lawrence.*

When not on tour, Dorothea Lawrence lived in the 1882 home that was built by her grandmother on Stelle Avenue. A great-grandniece of John Adams Dix and a direct descendant of Francis Scott Key, Lawrence enjoyed working and entertaining in her antique-filled home. Dorothea Lawrence died in 1979.

A 1st Vice President of Massey Concrete Products, Charles Gilman was a pioneer in the use of reinforced concrete, especially for culvert pipe, cribbing, and piling. A classmate of Franklin Delano Roosevelt and Clifford Holland, Gilman played an active role in community service, religion, and sports.

THE NATIONAL CYCLOPEDIA OF AMERICAN BIOGRAPHY

Charles Gilman lived in this stately Hillside Avenue home that had extensive gardens and a carriage house with chauffeur's quarters. At some point in its history, this Second Empire home was literally cut in half, then enlarged and remodeled into a fashionable Colonial Revival.

48

Named for his maternal grandfather, Judge Joseph Galloway Rowland of the Supreme Court of Delaware, Rowland Cox was a Princeton graduate. After settling in Plainfield, Mr. Cox served on the Plainfield Common Council, the Board of Governors for Muhlenberg Hospital, and Board of Trustees of the library. Mr. Cox became an internationally recognized expert in patent, copyright, and trademark law.

After graduating from Harvard Law School, Archibald Cox, son of Rowland, took over his father's business. In a well-known case, Archibald Cox established the right of Johnson & Johnson to use the Red Cross symbol as its trademark. *Courtesy of the Cox family.*

ARCHIBALD COX, 1997

Archibald Cox's eldest son, Archibald II, following in a tradition of excellence, went on to graduate magna cum laude from Harvard Law School and became Solicitor General of the United States, a Harvard faculty member, an expert in labor law, and the author of several books. Today, he is best remembered as the special prosecutor fired by President Richard Nixon in what became known as the Saturday Night Massacre. *Courtesy of the Cox family.*

The Archibald Cox senior family lived in this rambling Dutch Colonial-style home on Rahway Road. Designed by the architectural firm of White and White, the home provided spacious accommodations for the Cox family of seven children.

We have touched on only a few of the many outstanding individuals who contributed to making Plainfield the "Queen City" in the late nineteenth century. Their bricks and mortar legacy remains with us today and has become a visible force in the rejuvenation of this most interesting place.

CHAPTER FOUR:
A LIVING LEGACY

The spacious formal gardens of E. P. Thomas on Belvidere Avenue inspired this artist's rendering for a 1920s Chamber of Commerce promotional piece on Plainfield. The scene was not imaginary — it was real, and just one of many such enchanting spots throughout the city.

After a century of productive existence as Colonial breadbasket and Revolutionary commissary, the placid countryside between the Green and Cedar Brooks forged a new identity as a summer resort and playground for the wealthy. Still essentially rural, the community offered the beauty and healthful properties of an unpolluted environment to newcomers...newcomers with money. And its townsmen possessed all the gusto needed to develop businesses and services to sustain their new economy. Escapees from now-industrialized cities came knocking at the door, and the building boom was on. Up went the hotels and the summer homes...all within an hour's travel from New York.

Known as "Prospect Hill," this summer home was built in the 1870s by the Denton family on a sandy lane that turned into a quagmire during spring thaw. The lane would become Prospect Avenue, and the home's name proved symbolic as builders pressed on toward the wooded outskirts of the city, leaving streets and avenues dubbed Woodland, Evergreen, Hillside, Highland, Oakwood, and Forest Hill trailing in their wake.

The quintessential nineteenth century garden ornament, the mighty stag, reclines beside an admirer. Herds of iron statuary trailed across the lawns of palatial estates as Victorian fads and foibles followed the railroad into suburban territory and Plainfield had its share. Happily, pink flamingos were not yet in vogue.

To collectors of needlework, finding an early nineteenth century sampler in such pristine condition is rare indeed. Finding one connected to Plainfield is a coup. In 1847, eight-year-old Ann Edgars chose colors from her garden to stitch the floral borders of her sampler. Those flowers bloom today, as vibrant as the day her needle brought them to life. Whether conceived as a classroom exercise or a schoolgirl's whim, the vivid border is unique. *Courtesy of Thomas C. Diller.*

The blossoms billowing overhead may not be 'New Dawn' or 'Constance Spry', but they are certainly Plainfield's heirloom roses. Obviously the pride of the homeowner, the flowers she gathers must have filled the house with a heady fragrance.

The ladies of Hillside Avenue gather at the rear of the Wallace mansion where stone walls, laid dry by farmhands of an earlier day, enclose an old orchard in full bloom. Reminiscing about the neighborhood in which he lived from 1912 to 1935, Dale Warren remarks, "The postman…in October would help himself to a Russet apple or two from the surplus of windfalls on the lawn." Was this the source? Gardening is a longstanding tradition in the Hillside Avenue Historic District. On a Dunham map of 1878, we discover Denton's Nursery, with a residence and greenhouse clearly marked, filling the space between Hillside and Woodland Avenues, southeast of Prospect Avenue. Perhaps the site of "Prospect Hill" has been identified.

Clockwise from top left: The slopes where American patriots once fought the British were under a new assault. Residential development surged on into the Short Hills, the last bastion of unspoiled farmland on the outskirts of Plainfield, and a new decorative element entered local garden design. Water had long been a feature of the city's brook side gardens for obvious reasons. Rock now added a fresh dimension for reasons less obvious. Deposited as a terminal moraine at the end of the last ice age, the boulders forming the underpinnings of the Short Hills had ended their long journey. Eons later, they resurfaced as the bane of eighteenth and nineteenth century farmers and the delight of twentieth century landscapers.

A gentrified farmhouse enters a new phase of its existence. The house appears ancient, the hilly road has not been paved, a well house remains in place, but this is no longer a working farmyard. Land once allotted to husbandry has been transformed into a pleasure garden replacing a formerly utilitarian landscape.

Designed during the 1920s, the Albert Atterbury garden on Hillside Avenue mirrors the garden principles of Giggleswick (seen in the bottom left picture) — water, rock, and luxuriant bloom. The house rides the crest of the hill, with lawns and flower beds spilling down the slope toward the rooftops below in graceful waves of texture, punctuated with rare trees and shrubs.

Climbing roses clasp the home's trellised walls in a warm embrace and the basic bones of the garden have been preserved and enhanced by the gentle refinements of today's owners. Continuously cultivated for over three-quarters of a century, this urban Eden is truly one of Plainfield's living legacies—a legacy shared by many during house and garden tours.

"Giggleswick" seems to have started it all. Marjorie Elliott's 1989 treatise on the Giggleswick estate on Woodland Avenue dates the stone cottage of George and Ella Mellick to 1894, with a larger, medieval-style great hall added soon after, and describes the rock gardens developed with the help of Swiss engineers using huge boulders dug up from the property. "The cavities created by the relocation of these boulders formed pools that were filled with water… (where) one could swim, after a fashion." Spring bulbs, irises, peonies, wildflowers, lilies of the valley, and jack-in-the-pulpits swathed the landscape in naturalized plantings. Though the estate house was razed after a fire, an enclave of luxury condominiums arose on the site, incorporating many of the pre-existing garden features. Thus, a legend lives on.
Courtesy of Courier News – Bridgewater, New Jersey.

Water continued to cast its spell over the city's gardens—even the landlocked. A variety of pools and a man-made canal laid the groundwork for Waldorf Ulrich's park-like estate at the intersection of Plainfield and Stelle Avenues. Unlike the Atterbury restoration, these tranquil views of long ago linger only on film. Originally designed in homage to Plainfield's Green Brook gardens, the graceful scene has been replaced by a block of suburban homes.

As the twentieth century progressed, the Colonial Revival style had a great impact on Hillside Avenue architecture as new homes continued to infiltrate the remaining farms and summer homes at the base of the hills. Residences, in the guise of New England farmhouses, sea captain's mansions, and southern plantation homes expressed a growing appreciation of America's early architecture. A neo-Georgian manor illustrates one of the many classically-inspired residences to which the avenue is heir. And, the rear of the building is as impressive as the front.

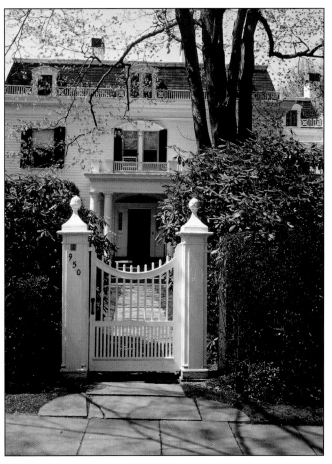

The gardens were as expansive as the homes, featuring balustraded terraces, picket fences, statuary, latticed follies, and surrounding hedges pierced by handsome gates. Dale Warren recalls, "However far and wide the summer may have taken me…the first sight of (home) with the September clematis fragrant over the front doorway was the best moment of all." New Orleans has its Garden District. Plainfield has its Hillside Avenue.

A vantage point from which to survey the scene was a welcome addition to any well-planned garden, and both of these restful spots were created on Hillside Avenue. This hideaway takes advantage of rock available on site as it curves around an old millstone forming pavement underfoot. The effect is rustic and woodsy, complementing the huge flowering azaleas and rhododendrons, boxwood, and ornamental trees in this private arboretum.

This second garden setting is much more formal. The curved bench is molded concrete with elaborate console armrests. Patterned brick forms the garden walk, binding tulips and a variety of seasonal spring bulbs into geometric beds. A handsome sundial forms a focal point where straight and curving lines converge. The basic elements survive intact, although the plantings have matured and changed around them. When last visited, the air in this sheltered nook was heavy with the scent of roses.

58

THE SHAKESPEARE GARDEN

When first discovered by Europeans, the Cedar Brook, smallest of the streams watering the plain, emerged from a cedar swamp below the 1684 Gordon home site on Brook Lane. A boon to the settlers and a welcome source of irrigation, over the centuries the brook has been channeled underground and out of sight until it springs to life again in the man-made basin of Cedar Brook Lake to form part of a public recreation area. Despite the lapse of 324 years, it makes its presence known as part of the Union County park system, site of Plainfield's lovely Shakespeare Garden, and scene of summer fishing derbys.

Established in 1927, the Shakespeare Garden was a joint project of the Shakespeare Society, the Plainfield Garden Club, and the Union County Park Commission to create a living tribute to the Bard of Avon. It was designed by the Massachusetts firm of Olmstead Brothers to include seventeen geometrical flower beds bounded by two 100-foot borders. Newly bedded out, this early view of the garden reveals the strong pattern devised by the Olmsteads.

In a recent photograph of the Shakespeare Garden, a vine-wreathed sundial forms a striking centerpiece. The topiary birds continue to flourish on their nests, and a sweeping view of open parkland marks the site of picnics and impromptu soccer games.

An old-fashioned paling fence separates the park's entry road from the garden, furnishing sturdy support for the roses and clematis that form a background for stately foxgloves and a wealth of summer bloom mentioned in Shakespearean verse.

Today's Shakespeare Garden is a vibrant floral tapestry, attracting both professional and amateur artists to the site. Not even humble clumps of spiderwort and Johnny-jump-ups, tucked into the garden's retaining wall, have been overlooked. An eighty-year-old heritage continues to weave its spell. *Courtesy of Pat Butynski, artist.*

Culling photographs for appropriate illustrations is the most enjoyable part of preparing a book like this. It can also leave one in a quandary. Does a particular dwelling qualify as a farm house or a town house? In the case of the Ginna residence, the choice could go either way. The house was erected for Daniel Ginna in 1902 on part of the property once the site of the circa 1862 Stephen Ginna "farm." The tract was once part of Cedar Brook Farm before the plantation was divided into residential lots. Across the street stand the stone pillars marking the lane to Senator Martine's homestead, just a block away.

In 1910, the Ginnas built an extension to the west front, later attaching a pillared, screened conservatory to its façade. A 1926 photograph displays the new construction. *Courtesy of Courier News – Bridgewater, New Jersey.*

In 1948, the Monday Afternoon Club purchased the mansion and, between 1949 and 1961, removed the open-air conservatory and altered the west wing to provide auditorium facilities. So it appears in a recent photograph and so it stands today, after conversion back into a family residence. The history of this gracious home has come full circle.

Daniel Ginna did not need to provide credentials as a country squire. He already owned Woodbrook Farms, a large dairy operation in the Oak Tree section of Raritan Township, now Edison. The home erected on Watchung Avenue was not on farmland per se, but its link to horticulture was undeniable. The earliest photograph extant of the Ginna mansion, pre-1910, seems to show greenhouses west of the residence. Despite a lack of any other visual or verbal confirmation of that fact, Ginna was widely known as the grower of championship chrysanthemums. A greenhouse for his prized plants would not have been beyond the realm of possibility.

CHRYSANTHEMUM DANCE.   *Langhorne, Photo.*

The Muhlenberg Hospital Auxiliary's fund-raiser in 1897 featured the "Spielkartenfest" or "card tournament," presenting the game of Whist with living cards. The Chrysanthemum Dance was a sprightly part of the festivities, celebrating the flower's growing popularity.

In this sepia view, the camera is poised to record the verdant backdrop of Mary Pickford's cinematic performance in the Plainfields. Then, as now, the lure of celebrity was hard to resist. *Courtesy of the Historical Society of Plainfield.*

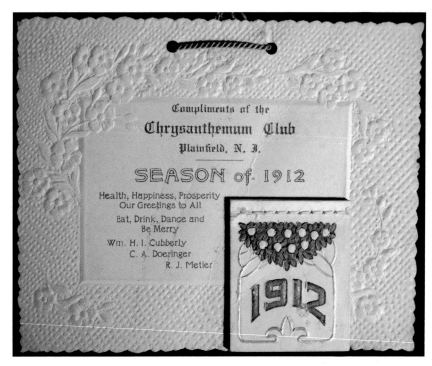

Compliments of the
Chrysanthemum Club
Plainfield, N. J.

SEASON of 1912

Health, Happiness, Prosperity
Our Greetings to All

Eat, Drink, Dance and
Be Merry

Wm. H. I. Cubberly
C. A. Doeringer
R. J. Metler

1912

Many gardens, both private and commercial, were beginning to specialize in a single genus of plants. Gladiolus, dahlias, and irises were close runners-up, but chrysanthemums appear to have held center stage in the Plainfields.

In the photographs that follow, another camera captures the garden created by a film crew for the wedding scene in Fox Searchlight's production of "Kinsey." The moviemakers of 1915 filmed their garden location as they found it while, in 2003, their counterparts hauled plants for their own location shoot on Stelle Avenue. The setting has been retained to write a new chapter in Plainfield's garden history. *Courtesy of Robin Gates.*

The September 1927 issue of *Country Life* contained a typical promotional advertisement for Plainfield home sites. It depicts a perfect world. The "war to end all wars" was over and the average citizen failed to acknowledge storm clouds gathering on the horizon. Similar storybook homes of the period are still to be found along the winding lanes of Plainfield's Sleepy Hollow neighborhood, although the carefree world in which they then existed was a fantasy. Their charm remains fixed in time like a wasp preserved in amber.

CHAPTER FIVE:
SOUNDS OF THE CITY

Today, as one hundred years ago, people live in a world of sound. The train whistle must have been an exciting sound, bringing people to visit from afar and taking people to explore new vistas.

Clockwise from top left:
John Maas, in *The Victorian Age*, states that "In the nineteenth century, the depot was a place of glamour and excitement and designed to look the part." Plainfield's Clinton Avenue station, along with the other three depots in town, confirms this statement.

The high-styled Victorian Netherwood station was the stopping point for the numerous summer vacationers who had a short five minute walk to the Netherwood Hotel. The depot was also convenient to the many New York businessmen who had chosen to build their handsome homes on the heights of Netherwood. *Courtesy of Sophie Dickson.*

After a fire destroyed the old station, a new stone structure of more modest proportions was built. Station master Erikson shown here bought a house nearby to be close to work. He was frequently commended for his aggressive maintenance of the new station. *Courtesy of Sophie Dickson.*

This cheerful looking group poses on a baggage cart in front of the North Avenue station. Railroads served as the hub of a community. It was not just the center for transportation, but the conduit for communication providing a link to the outside world.

65

The first high school in town was appropriately called Stillman School. When it opened in 1847, parents of school children were assessed one dollar per quarter if they were able to pay. Ring that bell! *Courtesy of the Historical Society of Plainfield.*

Trained as a physician, Dr. Stillman directed his considerable energies to civic affairs, especially education. As a founding father of one of the first public school systems in New Jersey, Stillman at various times, served as superintendent, trustee, and president of the Board of Education. *Courtesy of the Historical Society of Plainfield.*

OLD JACKSON SCHOOL HOUSE

How dear to this heart is the school of my childhood,
When fond recollection presents it to view!
The blue pail and dipper, the slab seats we sat on,
And the old hickory gad that we youngsters all knew;
The teacher's big arm-chair, the desk that stood by it,
And the stove, and the wood box we all had to fill.
O, the little old school house!
The storm-beaten school house!
The Old Jackson School House that stands o'er the hill!

Plainfield also had its own one room school house. The Jackson School, located near the corner of Terrill and Cushing Roads, stood for many years. By 1905, there was interest in preserving the building, but its ultimate fate is unknown. Both Col. Hand and the newspaperman, Arthur Brisbane, attended school here. *The poem is attributed to a member of the Hand family.*

Plainfield also boasted first class private schools including the Hartridge School for girls. The lower school was housed in this handsome Second Empire residence on West Seventh Street near Park Avenue. *Courtesy of the Wardlaw-Hartridge School.*

Hartridge took over the former Plainfield Casino, which provided expanded facilities for the upper school. The much altered old structure had a wonderful auditorium and the pleasantly furnished rooms provided a home-like atmosphere for boarding students. *Courtesy of the Wardlaw-Hartridge School.*

Not all days were occupied by study. The predecessor to the Hartridge School, the Randolph-Newton School, enjoys a picnic at Wetumpka Falls around 1889. *Courtesy of the Wardlaw-Hartridge School.*

In addition to a full course of study involving math, science, English, geography, Latin, Greek, and modern languages, the young men at Mr. Leal's School for Boys also had to practice military drill on the green in front of the Crescent Avenue Presbyterian Church. The purpose, Mr. Leal said, was "for the sake of securing grace and dignity of movement, erect carriage, and instant obedience to constituted authority." *Courtesy of the Wardlaw-Hartridge School.*

Theatricals were part of the curriculum, as well. At the very end of the nineteenth century, young shepherdesses gathered on the grounds of the Hartridge School for the annual spring pageant. *Courtesy of the Wardlaw-Hartridge School.*

Cheers and jeers must have punctuated the air of the competing baseball teams. In 1907, the Clinton Avenue Champs proudly displayed their trophies.

Sports were to become an integral part of school curriculum. At the Wardlaw Country Day School, successor to the Leal School, Charles Digby Wardlaw (standing to the left) felt that in addition to academic excellence, sports should be a part of the day, believing that "a restless boy is a mischievous one."
Courtesy of the Wardlaw-Hartridge School.

Just as much fun were the spontaneous games of marbles involving the younger set. In this photo, a group of enthusiasts play in the middle of a barely recognizable Prospect Avenue. *Courtesy of Mary Vic Griswold.*

The sounds of carpenters and masons disrupted quiet neighborhoods, but also heralded change and, in some cases, progress. In 1927, on the site of the former Lawrence tennis court, a brick colonial house was constructed for Mr. H. L. Harrison. The cost was $55,000.

By the end of the nineteenth century, Plainfield had both men and women's cycling clubs. However, a few years earlier, bicycles or velocipedes as they were then known were considered a pubic nuisance. An 1870s newspaper pointed its editorial finger in blame, stating, "A velocipede was seen on Cherry Street the other day with a man upon it. Where are the police?"

Park Avenue Baptist Church, Plainfield, N. J.

The pealing of many church bells ensured a joyful noise unto the Lord on Sunday mornings. Shown here are three of the many architecturally notable church buildings: Park Avenue Baptist, 1st Methodist Episcopal, and Trinity Reformed. Alas, all of these structures have fallen victim to urban renewal, shrinking congregations, and natural disasters.

TRINITY REFORMED CHURCH IN 1925

The 1788 Friends Meeting House has seen a lot of history pass by on Watchung Avenue. This still active and continuously used structure has been recently — and lovingly — restored. It bears the unique distinction of being the only eighteenth century building to survive in the commercial area.

A new trolley line was occasion for a "trolley opener." The clanging bell and fireworks would bring residents to their front porches to see the new suburban mode of transportation. In June 1900, the Arlington Avenue line opened and extended all the way to Woodland Avenue by Hillside Cemetery. The paper noted that the trolley ran through the potato and corn fields where suburban homes would one day be built.

Mechanized transportation meant fewer horses. Kensington Riding Academy stayed in business by promoting sport and exercise. Their ad stated that the beautiful scenery and bridle paths provided a "health-giving, brain-resting, and altogether delightful recreation." History would repeat itself again decades later when cruise ships competed against air travel for passengers. Does anyone recall the shipping industry slogan "Getting there is half the fun"?

Horse shows, an annual event in Plainfield, still continued to be popular and drew crowds to the Riding and Driving Club. The most notable difference was that spectators could now drive their new "gas guzzlers" to these equestrian events.

Yes, this is Plainfield, and there really were fox hunts here. This photo shows the back of Dr. Edward L. Finch's Park Avenue mansion where there is a lot of activity in preparation for the hunt. The hunts frequently took place on John Taylor Johnston's estate, which extended into the Watchung mountains and comprised over one hundred acres. The house viewed through the porte-cochere still stands, but has been unsympathetically altered. *Courtesy of Anne W. Finch.*

With eye upraised, his master's looks
to scan,
The joy, the solace, and the aid of man,
The rich man's guardian,
the poor man's friend,
The only creature faithful to the end.

Cars replaced horses, chauffeurs replaced groomsmen, and carriage barns became garages. Henry Talmadge's chauffeur, in his new conveyance, proudly poses in front of the old carriage house. The Talmadge mansion, which contained over thirty rooms, was a Belvidere Avenue landmark for many years. Both the house and carriage house were destroyed by fire in the late 1960s.

Driving a less glamorous model, George Strong's chauffeur poses by the family mansion on Central Avenue. *Courtesy of Lauren McCready.*

Why walk when you can ride?

Parades have always drawn crowds and sometimes resulted in an excess of decoration. Nevertheless, the festivities of these pre-television and pre-radio days were welcome events.

Two hundred and twenty six years after the first Scots established their plantations beside the Green and Cedar brooks, the MacKenzie Clan Fraternal Organization, in full regalia, strides briskly down Park Avenue toward the railroad underpass in this circa 1910-1912 photograph, adding the skirl of bagpipes to sounds of the city. *Courtesy of Jean Roxburgh.*

Servicemen, community groups, and city-supported services were all honored on parade days. Andy and Mack, the fire horses, get their ovations on Watchung Avenue. The house in the background is the site of today's YMCA.

On holidays such as Decoration Day, a local parade might precede a respectful visit to the cemetery, followed by a family gathering. On Decoration Day 1889, the Fritz Wiecher family poses in front of their West Seventh Street mansion. Top row — left to right: Ralph Wiechers, Henrietta Heerhold, L. Natalie Stirn, Louis Stirn, George Fred Wiechers, Professor Methfessel, Tante Heerhold. Lower row — Edmund Stirn, Elvira Methfessel, Mr. Detjens, Phillip Gossler, Mr. Rust, Antonia Methfessel, John Frederick Wiechers, Emily Wiechers, Lieschen Seeman. *Courtesy of Emila Carlson.*

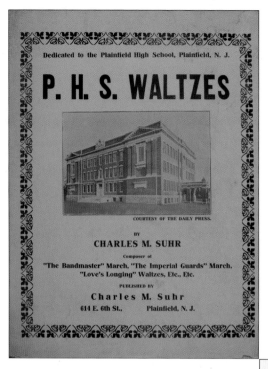

History does not record whether a special event precipitated this sheet music for Plainfield High School, but students and parents both must have been pleased by the singular recognition.

An inspiration for his generation as well as our own, memories of William H. Perrine still bring the muffled sound of drums to our city. Born in 1845, Perrine lived to witness the surrender at Appomattox when the heavy material of a cap he swapped with a friend deflected the bullet meant for him. New Jersey's last surviving Civil War veteran was laid to rest in Hillside Cemetery in 1945.

In a city of competing sounds, it is doubtful that the street clocks made much noise. However, in addition to displaying the time, these important pieces of street furniture provided visual reference points and signposts in a bustling downtown.

Chapter Six:
Mind Your Own Business

It has been said that people who do not mind their own business, have no business or no mind.

UNITED NATIONAL BANK

The Dr. John Crater Sutphen house on West Second Street, circa 1830-50, has been part of the downtown business scene since 1868 when Dr. Sutphen, fourth mayor of Plainfield, purchased the building as his home and medical office. The Plainfield Trust Company acquired the property in 1946, utilizing the site over the years (and through a number of name changes) to house a variety of banking departments until its closing in 2005 as the PNC Bank's Community Education Center. Part of the fabric of the city since before the Civil War, the Sutphen House tenaciously holds its ground. *Courtesy of Gail Hunton.*

An architectural monument whose very presence inspires trust and confidence, the former United National Bank building awed its patrons with the six fluted Ionic columns, marble lobby, and coffered ceiling. This formidable air of assurance is sadly lacking in new banks today. The pictured structure has been allowed to deteriorate and rumor says that ownership will be assumed by the City of Plainfield. It might be quicker and less painful to turn ownership over to enemy agents.

The forbidding gated entrance to the enormous vault allowed not only safe deposit boxes, but silver and valuables storage.

To be seen and not heard, the bank provided an elegant pilastered telephone booth. Unlike today's overbearing use of cell phones, the public then preferred to keep their private conversations private.

In pre-politically correct days, fashionable women wore fashionable fur coats. The fortress-like bank provided security as well as cold storage.

Swain's Art Store

Walter P. Swain succeeded his father in the business. He also succeeded in maintaining the business through two World Wars and the Depression. *Courtesy of Swain Galleries.*

Plainfield's oldest surviving commercial establishment is Swain's Art Store. Opened in 1868, the original sign on display today says Philip Swain Practical Gilder. *Courtesy of Swain Galleries.*

Through four generations of family ownership, Swain's has occupied several locations in the city. Many residents today still recall the West Front Street location with its signature crystal chandeliers in the display windows. *Courtesy of Swain Galleries.*

Today, Swain Galleries is operated by Ann Swain, daughter of Walter P. Swain, Jr., and occupies this Second Empire house in the Crescent Avenue Historic District. Listed on both the State and National Register of Historic Places, this home has been painted in a multi-colored palette highlighting its architectural elements. *Courtesy of Swain Galleries.*

This building on East Third Street, still standing today, operated as a meat packaging warehouse. For many years, it was the location of a popular restaurant called "What's Your Beef?"

As demand rose for commercially prepared food, new industries took root. This photo appears to be a bakery. The young women in their starched white aprons pause momentarily in the middle of a busy day. *Courtesy of Plainfield Public Library – Plainfield, New Jersey.*

The Plainfield Sign Company occupied this large brick building downtown on the block that would later be known as the Park Madison site. Maybe the pedestrians were unaware of the photographer or perhaps they were being directed to move along by the traffic officer on his umbrella-shaded podium.

For many years, prolific Plainfield photographer Paul Collier operated his studio downtown and produced postcards under the name "Star Company." His photographic legacy is invaluable to residents and historians.

Plainfield had any number of eating establishments. The lunch counter probably served shoppers — as well as businessmen in a hurry. The scale may have been an inducement to eat light.
Courtesy of Plainfield Public Library – Plainfield, New Jersey.

As Plainfield prospered, multi-use structures were erected downtown. The Jackson Building on the corner of West Front Street and Madison Avenue provided retail space on the first floor while the upper floors contained apartments with large awning-shaded windows.

The Post Office presented a handsome neo-classical façade on Watchung Avenue. The fine shade trees must have provided a welcome respite for pedestrians. Inside, visitors could admire two murals done by the Russian-born artist, Anton Refregier. *Courtesy of Plainfield Public Library – Plainfield, New Jersey.*

One early house, an antique itself, managed to survive into the twentieth century by selling antiques. Its honest architecture harks back to a pre-Gilded Age Plainfield. *Courtesy of Plainfield Public Library – Plainfield, New Jersey.*

This brick building with its numerous windows and Romanesque arch occupies a highly visible corner on North and Watchung Avenues. The houses in the background, now long gone, remind us of Plainfield's growing commercial prosperity. *Courtesy of the Historical Society of Plainfield.*

Established in 1898, the Marchant brothers ran the Plainfield Milk and Cream Company. Operating from 112 Watchung Avenue, the store also offered fresh eggs and butter.

This unusual building sports a pediment that looks like it was removed from a piece of furniture. Located on Sycamore Street, decorator C. H. Lane had his office here. A promotional ad for the business stated "the unskilled hand can mar the appearance of a building the same way that the appearance of a beautiful woman can be spoiled by an ill-fitting gown."

This West Second Street brick building with its stepped Flemish gable housed the Ivamy Market, which was billed as a high class meat market with all varieties of seafood. By 1916, their seafood products were kept fresher by the latest glass and porcelain-lined refrigerators.

Well into the twentieth century, ice cutting was an essential winter activity. After snow was scraped off the ice, it was cut into blocks and pulled from the water with iron hooks. The ice was then stored in "ice houses" and delivered as needed to local homes and businesses to preserve food during the warm months. The invention of the electric compressor effectively put an end to this arduous business.

A deep underground river provided water for the growing city of Plainfield. The sophisticated water works system was featured in an issue of *Scientific American*.

As the industrial age progressed, many drastic changes took place. Mechanization made the typewriter a reality and women began to enter the workplace. The pictured machine looks antique to us today, but before its invention scriveners had to tediously copy everything by hand.

Hotelier John Truell operated this unusual looking establishment well into the twentieth century. Providing rooms and family suites, this hotel consisted of several older homes joined together by additions and glassed-in companionways. The complex, located on Central Avenue, was destroyed by fire.

In the middle of the block on North Avenue stood the Hotel Kensington. Built in 1876, it offered forty sleeping rooms. By 1916, it was advertised as the best two dollars a night hotel in New Jersey.

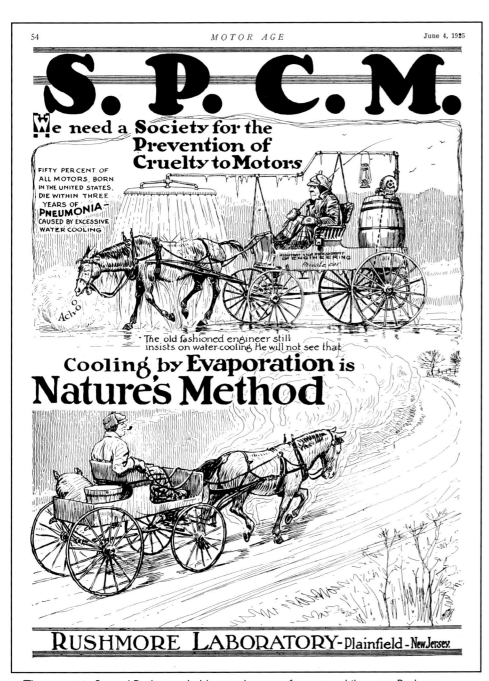

The eccentric Samuel Rushmore held several patents for automobile parts. Rushmore displayed a rare trace of humor in his magazine advertisement promoting an efficient cooling process for the automobile.

While studying at Cornell in 1903, Clarence Spicer patented his invention, the universal joint. Moving to Plainfield, Spicer opened a small factory to manufacture his invention. The universal joint quickly caught on and revolutionized the auto industry. Eventually, Spicer and other experts were called upon to design the Class B Liberty truck for Army use in World War I. Today, the Spicer Company exists under the name "the Dana Corporation."

This bustling downtown scene reminds us of the description of Plainfield put forth by the Federal Writers project. "Plainfield is a busy commuter's town with smart shops and substantial manufacturers."

This streetscape of Plainfield shows a downtown well on its way to becoming a city. Residences were being quickly swallowed up by commercial interests. The rural aspect of life was also disappearing as cars began to outnumber horse-drawn carriages.

CHAPTER SEVEN:
DOBBIN'S DOMAIN

In a period engraving, the residence of Seymour Hait, circa 1865-1870, rises from the past like a castle envisioned by the Brothers Grimm. The French mansard roof and tower, ornamental brackets, hooded dormers, and iron cresting are repeated on the windmill-topped carriage house behind the West Seventh Street home. The engraving permits a view of the Hait stable as it once was, and introduces similar buildings to follow, each with its own fairy-tale qualities.

In 1898, Edward H. Ladd, II chose one of the last remaining bits of Stelle farmland on which to build a handsome Neo-Georgian home. It was, and is, a vision of hipped roof, dentil course, corner quoins, arched and peaked dormers, and beautifully-detailed classical motifs. Possessing the means and taste to do so, he also erected a miniature version of the mansion to house his horses and driving equipment. The new estate was the talk of the neighborhood, and friends from Hillside Avenue were eager to visit.

Dorothea Dix Lawrence, niece of photographer Reina Lawrence, bats the birdie in the backyard of her home. The Ladd carriage house stands next door, all rigged out in its original hayloft doors and pulley, stall windows, carriage entrance, and the results of Monday's washday on the line. *Courtesy of the Plainfield Public Library – Plainfield, New Jersey.*

The pendulum swings and, sixty-odd years later, the carriage house itself became the topic of conversation on the street. Smaller families, rising costs, and the lack of household help now dictated more compact housing, and the conversion of sturdy estate outbuildings into living quarters was a viable alternative. Since the 1920s, many like-minded residents had followed that course, for carriage houses were plentiful in Plainfield's older residential districts.

Now fronting on Field Avenue, the Ladd carriage house preserves many of its original Georgian-style details, although the carriage entrance once piercing the eight-inch brick walls and railing-linked dormers have disappeared. The passage of 110 years "hath not staled (the stable's) infinite variety." *Courtesy of Michael J. Wroble.*

This vintage charmer on Hillside Avenue faces the twenty-first century essentially as it did when constructed; shingled exterior, domed ventilator skirted by a Chippendale-style railing, original doors and windows, and period fittings, including horse stalls, iron stall dividers, and well-used feeding troughs.

Can you identify this strange object? A foot stool, you say? Yes, but made of iron? Well, it is a carriage stool, the iron base designed to take abuse no self-respecting mahogany version would ever encounter in the parlor. Described many years ago by a lady whose husband drove carriages for a living, we accept the definition as gospel. And wonder how many have survived after stubbing toes in homes across America.

Rounding the corner of the carriage house just pictured on a sunny morning in 1912, Mrs. Warren handles the reins of her beautifully matched pair for a trip to a Muhlenberg Hospital Auxiliary meeting or a visit with the Ladds. Off they go for the day's activities. Giddyap, Peter! Get along, Paul!

Shared interests make good neighbors, for the nearby carriage house on Hillside Avenue has also been maintained in its original condition. A spacious board-and-batten exterior reflects the colonial styling of the home to which it belongs. A wing appears to have been constructed as servants' quarters or extra rooms for guests.

The guest house wreathed by boxwood and azaleas.

This Madison Avenue carriage barn served the Colonial Revival mansion on Central Avenue built for S. L. Schoonmaker, Esq. in 1904 and was purchased soon after by William Coriell. First converted in 1948 to provide living quarters on the second level with an artist's studio and classrooms below, the ground floor was later redesigned to provide a spacious family room. *Courtesy of William J. Santoriello.*

The hip-roofed, clapboard, and shingle structure with dentil cornice and wood fan on the south frontage displays appropriate colonial detailing and unusual six-over-one windows. Originally painted colonial gold to match the manor house, the barn acquired a dark brown façade by the 1960s. *Courtesy of William J. Santoriello.*

A period photograph from the Santoriello files and a circa 1983 image by Michael Wroble contrast the old carriage entrance with the new. The opening has been fitted with a modern door and window, but the original sliding doors have been retained on either side to bar access when desired. *(This house's story comes full circle with a more recent photograph appearing in the upper left corner of the next page.)*

The Madison Avenue façade of the Schoonmaker-Coriell carriage house has been newly revealed by removing the overgrown pines that obscured it (see pictures on previous page). Harking back to an earlier day, the exterior has been lightened by a fresh, café au lait paint job, announcing the most recent stage in its 104-year history.

A unique home on Randolph Road was transformed in 1963 from a neglected carriage house into the lovely residence of today. The carriage doors have been replaced by windows at the left of the entrance, and the hayloft doors have been glazed to light a two-story interior staircase. Although the lines of the original, ventilator-crowned stable remain unchanged, the varying rooflines of new extensions impart the charm of southern manor house dependencies to the whole.

Exterior doors are original, stall doors have been reclaimed for interior use, and portions of the old carriage entrance have been incorporated into a handsome entry gate. The pool has been positioned to reflect the house in its entirety and gardens illustrate the seclusion to be gained on the grounds of remodeled outbuildings.

A *Courier News* article once headlined "Carlton Mews" as, "Plainfield's most elegant hayloft." No one would ever argue the point. The carriage house of the Ginna estate was converted by the Lare family between 1921-1924, and beautifully renovated by Lucy and Raymond Rose in 1961. Many original features including the G-for-Ginna weathervane and tiles unearthed from a three-hundred-foot rose arbor along Carlton Avenue were preserved and recycled.

Throughout the Roses' tenure, Carlton Mews contributed its incomparable charm to the city's many charitable functions through architectural tours, a designer show house, and summer garden parties. That tradition continues today in a setting of floral abundance.

Our camera catches a view rarely seen in present-day Plainfield — the entrance to an old, brick-walled stable yard. Preserved by the Roses to provide a dining terrace outside the kitchen door, its narrow dimensions originally helped steady the horses during daily grooming sessions.

It's always a delight to come across original photographs of the subject one is researching, and this is one of those times. Here is a view of the car barn behind the Wallace house on Hillside Avenue, almost stark in its newness and showing the small appendage certainly constructed to house staff. The barn has now settled comfortably into its own special niche on Prospect Avenue as a private residence. *Courtesy of the Shortridge and Wallace families.*

A country gate marks the entrance to the building that once sheltered Mrs. Wallace's car — one of the first Model T Fords in town. A lovely sweep of ivy and apple trees carpets the approach to the single-story, shingled dwelling. Are the apple trees survivors of the orchard established here, or are they a subtle tribute to the farmer who planted that orchard a century or more ago? It doesn't matter. In spring, the ivy starred with daffodils beneath a blush of pink and white is its own reason for being.

A survey of Plainfield's fabled carriage houses is worthy of a book of its own, with a chapter dedicated to each conversion. No two chapters would be alike. None would embrace the concept of one-size-fits-all. All would catalogue stressful birth pangs. What follows is the story of just one: the Abbott carriage house. Witness the chaos.

Before and after photographs of both the front and rear elevations of the Abbott stable are self-explanatory. The unique exterior features have been retained, with a front entrance replacing a window in the tower. At the rear, new multi-pane doors and windows fill space where carriage doors once opened, the hayloft doors have given way to a windowed dormer, but the arched porte-cochere still shelters the drive to the home's hidden gardens.

The combination coach and gate house opening to the gardens of the Charles Abbott estate was erected around 1883. Originally attached to the main house that fronted on Central Avenue, this masonry and brick outbuilding with its Norman tower, Palladian window, and eye-catching ventilator was rescued in 1959 when the house was demolished, retaining a portion of the connecting link to balance the beautiful compound arch and preserve the curved windows.

Closure has been achieved. The Stelle Avenue entrance flaunts iron stall dividers recycled as doorstep railings, and welcomes visitors through the tack room decorated with old, iron hooks from which bridles and harnesses once hung. A magnificent horse chestnut showers petals on all who enter, a silent benediction on Bertha and Robert Raudebaugh who created and shared the home's history for more than forty years. We end our "Tale of a Carriage House" with a fine drawing of the post-conversion results.

In an old engraving of the Jacob Kirkner residence on West Eighth Street, a carriage house mirroring the elaborate architecture of the home's Queen Anne style holds its own against the competition. The mansion is gone now, replaced by modern homes. The coach house, a survivor of fickle fate, stubbornly refuses to yield.

The Kirkner carriage house, circa 1882, stood at the end of a carriage drive sweeping back from West Eighth Street. Now oriented toward Field Avenue, the untouched brick stable with clipped gable roof, diamond paned windows, and fish scale shingles occupies the rear of an adjoining property. With its mellow brick walls and copper-capped ventilator, this fanciful reminder of olden days still stops traffic on the street and inspires inquiries from passersby.

The quaint, shingled building on Thornton Avenue with its projecting, two-story tower was first listed as a residence in tax rolls of 1875. Prior to that time, it served as a carriage house and, as the story goes, may have been moved from its original site. The story rings true. Examine the engraving of the Hait House. If the French mansard roof and windmill were removed from the stable, the tower base bears an uncanny similarity to the truncated tower we see here.

This carriage house recreates the aura of a modest country cottage, but its site just beyond a pair of imposing estate gateposts flanked by ancient rhododendrons suggests it might also have served as the gatekeeper's cottage in its pre-conversion days. Today, it is refreshing to glimpse the sun-dappled stable in its private grove of trees on East Seventh Street. One enjoys a reminder of Plainfield's rural past hidden away on a busy thoroughfare.

"Cranehurst Mews," circa 1870, is straight out of a medieval fairy tale with its diamond-paned windows, brick arches, second-story overhang supported by masonry consoles, and hayloft doors. Converted in the 1930s, Dobbin's former home on Field Avenue boasts compact, low maintenance landscaping. No one in the neighborhood can fathom how a street side planting of hostas magically survives the city's de-icing crews.

Intact from brick foundation to rooftop cupola, this sturdy building across the way from "Cranehurst Mews" hosts an apartment above the garage. *Courtesy of Michael J. Wroble.*

This multi-dormered, windmill crowned carriage house, like none other in the city, still stands behind the Boardman Tyler mansion on West Seventh Street. What a sight it must have been in its glory days.

In later years, the roof was raised and altered to house an indoor squash court on the second floor. Also pictured is an amazing Palladian window installed to light the court—a window more suitable for a mansion than a stable. Woe to him who sent a ball smashing through that window in the heat of competition.

110

Plainfield's coach houses are an extra dividend from the Gilded Age and, like the mansions they served, were often remodeled to reflect current taste. During the Colonial Revival era, a three-bay structure at the bottom of a garden on Evergreen Avenue was the perfect choice for a copy of early American outbuildings sprinkled throughout the Connecticut countryside.

Local residents will recognize this site as the former home of a woman whose principles were as strong as her opinions. Her lifelong dedication to the city involved active service with eighteen civic, educational, cultural, and humanitarian organizations; from founding the Second Street Youth Center to volunteering as a nurse's aide at the Muhlenberg Regional Medical Center. Today, the Anne Louise Davis Room at the Plainfield Public Library honors her devotion to the community.

A portrait of Anne Louise Davis has a pensive air. It speaks to us of solid, American values — courage, candor, and clean windows. *Courtesy of F. Edgar Davis.*

A painted brick, Queen Anne coach house tucked away behind the equally-colorful Catherine Webster residence, formerly a home for gentlewomen on Franklin Place, is little changed from the days of haylofts and hitching posts.

A substantial masonry and brick stable with majestic fan window rises beside the Van Wyck Brooks mansion on West Eighth Street, accompanied by a bracketed, frame laundry just visible through the trees. An unequaled collection of outbuildings may still be found along Plainfield's streets.

This board and batten, bracketed example also survives at the junction of Woodland and Highland Avenues. It displays the starchiness of a prim Victorian bodice with a flash of lace at the collar.

113

This colonial-style cottage built in 1928 on Randolph Road is not a carriage house, but after its purchase by a new owner in 1937, a legend began to grow. The homeowner had been raised at "Fernstone," a circa 1892 mansion on West Eighth Street, two blocks away from her current address. Over time, the family carriage house had been demolished, but never forgotten by the girl who played there as a child. Perhaps the home in which she lived rekindled childhood memories. Did it happen that way?

In truth, the home's interior does not reflect a typical 1920s floor plan. While the house is otherwise compact and space-efficient, the ceiling of the living room has been raised to the rafters to accommodate a staircase rising to the second floor, strongly reminiscent of many an old coach house stairway connecting the carriage room below with the hayloft above. If the home was altered to recreate the appearance of a long-lost treasure, the vision was realized. It is a charming house and a charming legend.

Behind a splendid old azalea hedge on West Eighth Street slumbers a half-timbered Tudor carriage house. When the Van Wyck Brooks Historic District's first carriage house tour took place in 1983, the building, just as it appears here, was featured as ripe for conversion. A year later, a housewarming introduced new owners to the neighborhood amidst specimen trees and shrubbery. *Courtesy of Michael J. Wroble.*

CHAPTER EIGHT:
COSMETIC SURGERY

Our built environment is frequently transformed. The results can be horrifying or gratifying depending on your point of view. *Courtesy of Ralph Attanasia, a student at du Cret School of the Arts.*

Looking positively bucolic in its leafy setting of Japanese red maples, pines, and oaks, the Childers' home on Park Avenue and Sixth Street was a holdout to downtown development. Based on a "bash and build" mentality in the 1980s, the home succumbed to the wrecking ball. Its replacement – well, you be the judge. *Courtesy of the Lane family.*

A Chamber of Commerce promotional featured the stately Wilbur Drake home on Woodland Avenue. Crowning the hilltop like a Greek temple, its enclosed third floor belvedere afforded a spectacular view of the Watchung Mountains. After sitting abandoned and in disrepair for many years, the home was demolished and twenty-five, yes count them, new homes were constructed on the site. Not a single one of the cookie cutter replacements took advantage of the desirable setting.

Sometimes older homes are lost, but the replacements are gratifying. This nineteenth century structure, located on Rahway Road, may have appeared quite dated in the early twentieth century. In 1930, Christie Hamilton had the house removed and built a spectacular period revival confection of brick, stone, and half timbering. Visible in the foreground is the old hand water pump from the original house...the lone sentinel harking back to an earlier time. *Courtesy of Richard Loosli.*

Many remodelings are undertaken just for fashion's sake and the old form is encased in a new skin. In the 1920s, *House Beautiful* magazine demonstrated how this Belvidere Avenue Victorian home could be transformed into a trendy Tudor Revival.

Adding impetus to the Colonial Revival trend was the restoration of Colonial Williamsburg. Although handsomely remodeled with balustraded roofline, swan's neck pediment, and corner quoins, the mansard roof proclaims this as a circa 1870 home. To complete the picture, this distinguished Seventh Street house also had a boxwood parterre outside the oval dining room.

Yes, it's the same house. Into the Plainfield pantheon of bad taste goes this 2008 remuddling. Historic preservation, a vital force in Plainfield for almost thirty years, takes a giant step backward. A bouquet of onions goes to this stinker!

Sometimes harmonious alterations are made that are completely sensitive to the original structure. This Shingle Style home on Hillside Avenue was added onto in the early twentieth century. It not only kept its original character, but it provided the owner with the necessary space for his growing family. Note the mini Palladian window on the third floor...a gesture to the then popular Colonial Revival style.

Today, as in the nineteenth century, West Eighth Street is lined with many magnificent Victorian era and Colonial Revival mansions. This Second Empire residence was moved across the street and stuccoed. Its original detailing remained intact and the home serves as a handsome addition to the VanWyck Brooks Historic District.

120

The S. L. Schoomaker house on Central Avenue was built circa 1904 in the "modified style of colonial architecture." The architect E. G. W. Dietrich was called upon in a few years of completion to enclose a portion of the wraparound porch. The pages of Scientific American Building Supplement showed how to tastefully accomplish this end. The only question remaining is: Did the owner really need another room?

House at Plainfield N.J.

E. G. W. Dietrich
Architect
New York

Dining Room in House at Plainfield N.J. E. G. W. Dietrich Architect 18 Broadway N.Y.

Architect Dietrich also obliged the owner by creating a visionary concept of how the dining room would look in the completed dwelling.

In the nineteenth century, often times brick houses were constructed of a softer grade of brick that was intended to be painted. In the twentieth century, homeowners, thinking they were doing the right thing, had the paint removed using the recommended method of sand blasting. Unfortunately, this process pitted the brick and exposed its soft inner core to the elements, causing further deterioration. One such example is the fine Orville T. Waring home on Park Avenue shown in the nineteenth century and again undergoing this destructive process.

An integral design element in Victorian era building is the front porch. Visually, they were not only decorative, but they anchored the house to the ground, breaking up the strong verticality. On another level, porches were functional, providing the owners with a roofed summer living room and shading the interior from the hot sun in pre-air conditioning days. Over the years, porches deteriorated and became expensive maintenance issues. Their removal brought to the forefront the importance of their visual contribution. See for yourself in the two pictured examples, the first pair on Crescent Avenue; the second on Madison Avenue.

Kubla Khan may have decreed a "pleasure dome," but I'll bet he did not reckon with the advent of the twentieth century tin man. In this monstrous monument to insensitivity, the former home of Solomon Solis Carvalho on West Eighth Street and Central Avenue lost all its trim and got canned.

In another example, this poor West Seventh Street house lost its hat, shutters, and much of its trim, now concealed under a vinyl coat.

If this vintage photo had not been labeled "Our Front Street Home," it might have been difficult to locate in its recast appearance. Someone should have heeded that old adage, "If it ain't broke, don't fix it."

YIKES!

Do any remuddlings get reversed? You bet they do. This Shingle Style house on Stelle Avenue had its modernizations stripped away and today looks much as it did when first built.

This Arlington Avenue home was built in 1875. In 1905, the house was extended on the north and south frontages, but the caring owner regrouped the decorative brackets to fit the new format. Kudos to the unnamed individual.

This dwelling started life as a shelter for sheep on the 1882 Jacob Kirkner estate on Field Avenue, and was remodeled as a New England cape in 1939. The home is true to the architect's vision and to its original tenants. An old watering trough remains in the barnyard, while the orchard's lone survivor blooms anew each spring.

BIBLIOGRAPHY

Commemorative Book Committee. *Plainfield 300 Years, 1684 – 1984*. Upper Montclair, New Jersey: Josten's Incorporated, 1987.

Elliott, Marjorie Blackman. *Giggleswick*. 1989.

Honeyman, A. Van Doren. *History of Union County, N.J., 1664 – 1923*. New York, New York: Lewis Historical Publishing Company, 1923.

Hooker, Ralph Moreton, and Rev. A. H. Lewis. *Plainfield, New Jersey*. Plainfield, New Jersey: *The Plainfield Daily Press*, 1895.

Hunton, Gail. Survey of Historic Building Resources for the City of Plainfield. Plainfield, New Jersey: 1985.

Smiley, F. T. *History of Plainfield and North Plainfield*. Plainfield, New Jersey: *The Plainfield Courier-News*, 1901.

Spies, Stacy E. *Images of America-Edison*. Charleston, South Carolina: Arcadia Publishing, 2001.

Taylor, Edward W. *Reflections of Old Plainfield*. Plainfield, New Jersey: 1976.

Veit, Richard F. *Images of America-South Plainfield*. Charleston, South Carolina: Arcadia Publishing, 2002.

Wardlaw-Hartridge School. *Strength from our Roots*. Warren, New Jersey: Sahlman Art Studio, 1996.

Warren, Dale. "As It Was Years Ago in Plainfield." *A Magazine of New Jersey History*. Proceedings of the New Jersey Historical Society: April 1965.

We know where these houses are. Do you?